Boulder Urban Trails

another book in the *Take A Bike!* series

also by Glen Hanket:

Underwear by the Roadside: LitterWalk
Coast-to-Coast

*-- the story of Glen and his wife Susan, who spent twelve months
walking from Maine to Oregon, bagging four tons of litter and
discovering the 'real America'.*

Take A Bike! A Guide to the Denver Area's
Urban Trails (2nd Edition)

-- Winner of the 2003 CIPA Evvy Award

and the books of the *Take a Bike* series:

- **Boulder Urban Trails**
- **Broomfield/Boulder County Urban Trails**
- **Adams County Urban Trails**
- **Westminster Urban Trails**
- **Jefferson County Central Urban Trails**
- **Jefferson County South Urban Trails**
- **Denver/Platte Triangle Urban Trails**
- **North Denver/Aurora Urban Trails**
- **Arapahoe County Urban Trails**
- **Highlands Ranch Area Urban Trails**
- **Douglas County Central Urban Trails**
- **Northern Colorado Urban Trails**
- **Southern Colorado Urban Trails**
- **Mountain Resorts Urban Trails**
- **Western Colorado Urban Trails**

Boulder

Urban Trails

another book in the *Take A Bike!* series

CAK Publishing _____

PO Box 953   Broomfield, CO 80038

Published by CAK Publishing, PO Box 953, Broomfield CO 80038

Catalog-in-Publication

Hanket, Glen
    Boulder County urban trails : another book in the take a bike! series / by Glen Hanket. – 1st ed.
    p. cm..
    Includes index.
    ISBN: 0-9709815-3-8

    1. Bicycle touring—Colorado—Denver. 2. Bicycle trail—Colorado—Denver. 3. Bicycle trail—Colorado—Boulder County. 4. Denver—Guidebooks. I. Title.

GV1045.5.C6H36 2001   796.64'09788
                                 CKI01-64067

Printed in Canada

This book is dedicated to

Mrs. Bostrom

My sixth grade teacher at Columbine Elementary school, who encouraged me to write.

Special acknowledgement to

Marni Ratzel

Bicycle trail planner for Boulder .

Thanks for the help!

Table of Contents

Introduction

Ahhh, to spend an hour two-wheeling – what could be finer? Feeling the sun on your face and a breeze at your back, passing under a canopy of trees, listening to birds sing – at these times, the problems of the world are miles away.

But you don't need to be – miles away, that is. For the Denver metro area hosts an extensive network of bike trails. Forget about needing a full day to take a simple ride – pack a lunch, load the bikes onto the car, drive an hour into the mountains, whoops! Time to drive back already. Instead, hop on a short trail near your home, or explore one of the long trails snaking through the metroplex.

The climate in Colorado encourages sports like bicycling. Even during the dead of winter snow rarely lasts, and dry, sunny days make it easy to get your exercise without spending your time inside a club. This region has had a love affair with bikes for many years. In 1900, reported the Denver Post, the city had more bikes per residents than any other US city.

However, automobiles pushed bikes out of the spotlight, and many years passed with no emphasis on bike facilities. Isolated trails existed in widely-spaced parks, or ran a short distance along Cherry Creek, but no network existed. Then the South Platte River flooded in 1965, sparking interest in converting it from an eyesore to a public treasure – which included bike trails running its length.

In June 1974 Mayor Bill McNichols appointed Joe Shoemaker chairman of the Platte River Development Committee. With a few hand-picked members, he tackled the transformation of the river. City dumps became parks, and dams soon sported boat chutes. By mid-1975, the first segments of the Platte River Greenway had opened, followed by the dedication of Confluence Park that September.

Now over thirty years have passed, and over five hundred miles of trails weave through the metropolitan area. Some offer steep pitches for a workout; others meander along lazy streams. No matter what style you prefer, there is bound to be something for you.

Before you take your ride, though, remember that biking can be dangerous. Always keep safety in mind, from the equipment you wear (yes, helmets can save lives!) to the traffic you ride in. Keep alert for pedestrians sharing your trails, and check both ways when crossing busy streets. At most major boulevards, a crossing light is available nearby.

R*ules of the Road*

So you've reached the trailhead. Now you're ready to fly down the pavement, setting a new land speed record, right?

WRONG!

One of the biggest challenges facing trail users is retaining the right to use those trails. Not everyone welcomes trails in their area, and many people actively fight to have them removed from their neighborhoods. They cite out-of-control bicyclists injuring bystanders or hikers trashing public lands as ammunition in their fight against the paths. Unless we're all careful, a few thoughtless individuals could make us lose the wonderful paths we enjoy.

To prevent that, trail users have adopted the 'rules of the road'. The ten common-sense rules:

1. Cyclists and skaters should yield to horses and hikers.

2. Cyclists and skaters should maintain control at all times. This means keeping your speed within reasonable limits, and slowing down when approaching blind curves.

3. Obey all signs and postings.

4. Respect private property. Close any gates you opened, and don't damage someone's land.

5. Wear a helmet when cycling and pads when skating.

6. Do not obstruct a path by stopping in the middle of it.

7. Always walk or ride on the right.

8. When passing someone, call out to warn them.

9. Do not litter!

10. Use extra caution when wearing headphones. You may not hear someone coming from behind.

Remember that you are sharing these paths with other users. Be an ambassador of good will! Something as simple as saying "Good morning" or "Good afternoon" as you pass someone goes a long way to brightening their day, and breaks down the stereotype of the 'rude cyclist'.

How to use this book

All trails in this book may be ridden with any type bicycle; no single- or double-track trails are included here. Most of the trails are also suitable for in-line skaters – check the

'Surface' description on the top of each writeup to insure that it is hard-surfaced. (However, some of the paved paths may be too weathered for a comfortable ride.) Of course, any of these trails are appropriate for a short walk.

In each writeup, special font styles call out convenient **<u>trailheads</u>** (usually city parks), ***other trails***, and *on-street bike routes*.

Certain maps include symbols to describe landmarks you may pass. The symbols and meanings are:

	city hall; university		golf course
	Gardens		parking / trailhead
	Library		hospital
	ball fields		tennis courts
	school		swimming
	post office		playground

Trails Overview

Boulder anchors the northwestern corner of the Denver metropolitan area. The area has always embraced bicycling (do you remember the Red Zinger Bike Race, and packs of speeding cyclists plying the Morgul Bismarck course?), and has led the way for counties preserving open spaces. Small wonder, then,

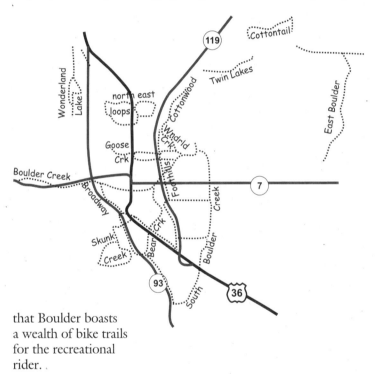

that Boulder boasts a wealth of bike trails for the recreational rider.

The trails, both paved and soft-surface, offer a variety of venues and vistas. A web of trails running through the city presents many chances for a loop trip. Some paths run along creeks or by lakes, others tour neighborhoods, and still others parallel major roadways (providing an excellent resource for bike-commuting).

Not all of the trails lie within city limits. The *East Boulder Trail* runs through open space east of Gunbarrel, by agricultural preserves and the scenic White Cliffs area. West of there, the *Twin Lakes Trail* plies a creekside corridor between unincorporated tracts, while to the north the *Cottontail/Homestead Trails* trace the edges of the Gunbarrel subdivision and connect to trails in Niwot.

Many trails lie in the northern reaches of the city. The *Wonderland Lake Trail* tours open spaces at the base of the city's northern foothills, connecting with the trail running through the *Four-Mile Creek Open Space*. Centennial Middle School (the author's alma mater) can serve as the base for a neighborhood loop trip using the *Wonderland Creek Greenway*. One leg of the greenway trail also provides a return path for the *Four-Mile Creek loop*, located in the northeast corner of town. The Four-Mile Creek trail ends one railroad track away from the *Cottonwood Trail*, which runs through undeveloped county land north of Hayden Lake.

You can take the *Goose Creek Trail* from central residential areas to the eastern fringes of the city. By linking the *Pearl Pkwy Trail*, you can execute a loop trip in the lands north of the old Crossroads Mall. These trails also provide access to the new Valmont Park and the eastern incarnation of the *Wonderland Creek Greenway*.

Bicycle commuters make good use of the trail paralleling the *Foothills Pkwy*, running four miles north-to-south through the town's eastern portion. It crosses Boulder's premier trail, the *Boulder Creek Trail,* which runs along the tree-shaded creek from Valmont Rd into *Boulder Canyon*. If you're looking for a loop, combine the Boulder Creek Trail with the *Broadway and Bear Creek* paths to tour a chunk of south Boulder. If you add the Broadway Trail to the creek path and the *Turnpike Trail*, you have another nice loop trip.

Boulder Creek isn't the only lush creek hosting a path. From that path's downstream end, the *northern South Boulder Creek Trail* runs by high-tech business parks and country-club homes on its way to the East Boulder Community Center. At that point, the soft-surfaced *southern South Boulder Creek Trail* runs through county open space with unobstructed vistas to the foothills. Connections along the Broadway, Bear Creek and Centennial trails allow you to form a *South Boulder Loop*. And if you want a short but strenuous ride, the *Skunk Creek Trail* climbs into the foothills behind the NIST complex on S Broadway.

Quiet neighborhood off Centennial Trail

Boulder Creek Trail/Boulder Canyon

DISTANCE: 3.2 miles off-street

SURFACE: concrete, gravel

DIFFICULTY: moderate — climbs in the canyon

DESCRIPTION:

Boulder's best-known trail must be the path following Boulder Creek through town. If you remember it most for its crowds, though, you're missing a trick. The extension of the trail into Bolder Canyon is much less traveled - and as a bonus, it will give you a better workout.

Though you could start this ride anywhere along the trail, we will choose Broadway as our milepoint 0.0. You can reach this point by following the Broadway Trail down from CU, or riding the creek trail behind Boulder High School, my alma mater.

After crossing under Broadway, pass behind the old courthouse and by the **Boulder Public Library**. If you're riding here in late spring, you're likely to see inner tubers playing in the cold waters. The path passes under 9th St at mile 0.3 and circles around Kid's Pond, where the tykes fish. Again, several dirt side paths let walkers and joggers escape into the trees. At 0.5 miles you cross under 6th St and pass by the Justice Center - be thankful you don't have business inside. On the far side of the Center, take a moment and look at the xeriscape garden.

A bridge at mile 0.9 crosses the creek and dumps you into **Eben G. Fine Park**, at the gateway to Boulder Canyon. (Restrooms are unlocked here in season.) This is a popular park with picnickers and people playing in the creek, and works well as a trailhead. As you follow the trail into the canyon, it passes a kayak course – during runoff season you can watch athletes practice their strokes. The trail now begins to climb, not steeply but consistently. It crosses a private driveway at mile 1.3, then crosses under Highway 119 at mile 1.9.

As the trail exits the tunnel, it turns to gravel. Though the surface is still well-graded, it is not recommended for road (skinny-tire) bikes. After passing a cliff popular with rock climbers, it crosses the creek and heads further up canyon. Another bridge at mile 2.9 recrosses the creek, and the trail finally ends at mile 3.2.

OPTIONS:

See *Boulder Creek Trail* for the extension of the creek trail east. You can also head up the Broadway Trail and take the *Bear Creek* or *Foothills Pkwy Loop.*

OTHER ATTRACTIONS:

One of Boulder's best-known attractions is the **Pearl Street Mall** (remember seeing it on *Mork & Mindy?*). The city turned the street running through the heart of downtown into a pedestrian mall in 1982, in order to revitalize the city center. It worked! Turn of the century buildings house a wide variety of merchants and restaurants. Shoppers can come for the goods, to people watch, or catch the buskers (street performers) and musicians entertaining the crowds.

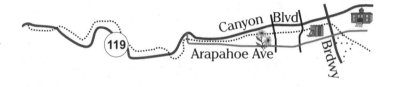

If history turns you on, downtown is the place to be. The **Downtown Boulder Historic District** showcases late-19th/early-20th century buildings in Queen Anne, Romanesque, Italianate and other styles. Headlining the list is the 1909 **Hotel Boulderado**, popular for banquets and weddings. Nearby is also the **Mapleton Hill Historic District**, with distinctive large homes dating back to 1865. Call Historic Boulder, Inc at 303-444-5192.

You can also browse through the art collection or the traveling exhibitions at the **Boulder Public Library**. Call 303-441-3100.

Boulder Creek Trail

DISTANCE: 4.0 miles off-street

SURFACE: concrete

DIFFICULTY: easy

DESCRIPTION:

Boulder is an ideal town for bicycling. Trails weave throughout the city, running both north-to-south and east-to-west. Bike shops abound, and health-conscious residents go out in most any weather. Of all the trails they use, perhaps the most popular is the Boulder Creek Trail.

The eastern end of the trail is the easiest to reach. Starting at Valmont Rd just east of 57th St, the trail starts by circling the north and west edges of a pond, running beside 57th St. At the far edge of the pond the trail forks (0.3), with the left branch following *South Boulder Creek*. For this ride, take the right branch upstream. It crosses over Boulder Creek in the shadow of a another red-brick industrial box imprisoning scores of technology workers, and quickly passes under 55th St (0.5).

Enjoy a short stretch along the creek, then ride along another pond in the open space bordering Pearl Pkwy. Ignore the right fork turning up *Goose Creek* (0.9), but take the left branch again when the path splits at mile 1.2; the straight-ahead route continues along *Pearl Pkwy*. The main path keeps open space to the left as it returns to the creek, crossing under the railroad tracks as it works its way west. The forested area around the creek has many side paths for walkers and joggers; workers from area companies may find an unused log for an impromptu picnic.

The trail briefly joins the *Foothills Parkway Trail* at 1.7 miles; to the right it runs back to Pearl St and beyond. Follow it to the left as it crosses the creek, then hang right at mile 1.8 as the *Foothills Parkway Trail* continues south. Our trail dives

11

under Foothills Pkwy then continues below street level, crossing under Arapahoe at mile 2.0. To the south the land is open, part of the CU athletic complex. The *Skunk Creek Trail* to your left leads into this area, but bear right instead. A greenhouse signals the end of open space, and soon you're pedaling behind residences.

After crossing under 30th St (2.5) and then over the creek, <u>Scott Carpenter Park</u> sits on your right. This park is popular year-round, for the sledding hill in the winter and the swimming pool in the summer, and for the skate park any time the weather is nice. (A right fork at the park's edge connects with the 29th St shopping district.) Past the park, the trail again has houses and businesses to one side. However, the creek always stays semi-wild, with large trees providing shade on hot days. Cross under 28th St at mile 2.8, and watch out for the

Valmont Rd

Pearl Pkwy

55th St

157

Arapahoe Ave

28th St

30th St

7

foot traffic from the Millenium Hotel and the people enjoying the tennis and volleyball courts by the trailside. Continue west, passing under Folsom St at mile 3.1.

Now the land rises steeply across the creek, and university buildings perch atop the hill. The trail passes by nice homes beneath the bluff as it heads west. At one point it splits into two one-way lanes as it passes a day-care area. It jogs sharply to cross under 17th St (3.7), emerging behind Boulder High School. A short time later it passes the football field, then burrows under Arapahoe again. On the adjacent street, a farmer's market peddles fresh produce during the summer. At this point, you can continue up into *Boulder Canyon*, or follow the *Broadway Trail* up to CU.

OPTIONS:

See *Skunk Creek/Bear Creek* or *Foothills Pkwy Trail* for details on loop trips that combine the Boulder Creek Trail with other Boulder trails. Also, you can branch from the trail on the west side of 28th St. An access trail/sidewalk runs beside 28th from Arapahoe to the campus, highlighted by public art. (You can see a nature island, the Flatirons Wall, or the Magic Bus Arch.) At Arapahoe, you can cross both roads to reach the new 29th St shopping complex.

OTHER ATTRACTIONS:

Have a hankering for art? The **Boulder Museum of Contemporary Art** at 1750 13th St presents newer art forms in a former warehouse. The 10,000-square-foot museum shows works of local, national, and international artists, and the upstairs theatre presents cutting-edge music and dance recitals as well as traditional theater productions. Call 303-443-2122.

Next to the Museum of Contemporary Art lies the **Dushanbe Teahouse**. This cultural attraction is a gift from Boulder's sister city in Tajikistan. It took more than 40 Tajik artists to create the decorative hand-painted and hand-carved ceilings, tables, stools, columns, and panels. Come in to see the Fountain of the Seven Beauties, eat food from around the world, or sip one of the 80-plus varieties of tea.

In Eben G. Fine Park

13

B roadway/Bear Creek Loop

DISTANCE: 7.5 miles, 7.0 miles off-street

ON-STREET: two residential stretches

SURFACE: concrete

DIFFICULTY: easy ride, with one hill

DESCRIPTION:

Boulder's trails get used extensively. Recreational riders pedal around town, students use bikes to reach classes, and commuters depend on them to get to work. This particular loop ties together downtown (via Boulder Creek), the University, and Table Mesa.

Start logging miles at Boulder Creek and Arapahoe Rd, just west of Boulder High. Instead of taking the creek trail under Arapahoe, take the sidewalk over the creek, then bear left then right. The path quickly climbs up University Hill, passing above Recht Field (the high school football stadium). Shift into low gear, but don't worry – the hill is short, and is the only real climb on the loop.

At the top of the hill, cross University Ave at the light. Ignore side trails leading into the campus, and keep Broadway close to your side. Slow down as you pedal through the university grounds – despite three lanes of trails, this area is very busy with student traffic. Check out the sandstone buildings of CU as you coast by; they are quite impressive. The trail continues skirting the campus, crossing Euclid Ave (0.7 miles) and Regent Dr (1.0) at traffic lights.

The trail now drops away from Broadway, reaching a fork at mile 1.2. Turn right and tunnel under Broadway. After crossing Baseline (1.4) the trail joins *Sunnyside Ln*, a short residential street that ends at mile 1.6. Just before the trail re-forms, a tunnel takes trail users under Boadway along *Skunk*

14

Creek. For this loop, ignore the tunnel and parallel Broadway along the trail across NIST (Bureau of Standards) property. (Parallel trails keep bikers and joggers separate.) This trail ends for good at the Dartmouth Ave light (2.3), but the bike route continues on *Harvard Ln* to Table Mesa Dr (2.6).

Cross under Broadway into **Martin Park**, a well-kept grassy expanse. After crossing under Martin Dr (3.0) the trail is squeezed, with concrete in the channel and fences on either side. It quickly passes under Moorhead Ave (3.2) and US36 (3.3), emerging into Open Space land. Ignore the *Turnpike Trail* crossing this one, and instead head north through the Open Space along tree-lined Bear Creek. There has been construction going on here for some time, and the trail has been relocated.

At 3.8 miles you cross under Baseline, entering another residential area. Tight curves are your latest concern as the trail passes under Gilpin Dr (3.9), and then coasts by a set of condos. You tunnel beneath Aurora Ave at 4.3 miles and roll through another park before this trail dead ends into an east-west trail (4.5). A right turn takes you to the *Foothills Parkway Trail*; turn left instead.

Cross Monroe Dr at 4.7 miles, then bear right at the school yard (4.8) to head toward Skunk Creek. The trail takes a sharp right at Colorado Ave (5.0), then crosses under the street (5.1). Following Skunk Creek, it tunnels under Discovery Dr into the CU Research Park. Surrounding you is an undeveloped area, accented by several ponds. This side trail ends at mile 5.4, when it joins the Boulder Creek Trail at Arapahoe Ave just west of Foothills Pkwy. Turn left here, and follow the Boulder Creek Trail (mile 2.0 in that writeup) west to return to your starting point.

OPTIONS:

You can ride or walk into the CU campus, exploring its grounds. If you want an alternate route to County open space, head south of town: after the ***Bear Creek Trail*** crosses under Broadway, cross Table Mesa Rd and head southeast on the bike route 1.4 miles to reach the ***South Boulder Creek Trail***.

OTHER ATTRACTIONS:

The CU campus is home to more than just students. Are you looking for recreation? The **University Memorial Center (UMC)** has a bowling alley, bookstore, and video games.

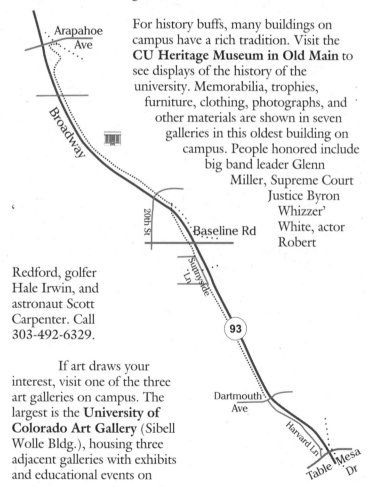

For history buffs, many buildings on campus have a rich tradition. Visit the **CU Heritage Museum in Old Main** to see displays of the history of the university. Memorabilia, trophies, furniture, clothing, photographs, and other materials are shown in seven galleries in this oldest building on campus. People honored include big band leader Glenn Miller, Supreme Court Justice Byron Whizzer' White, actor Robert Redford, golfer Hale Irwin, and astronaut Scott Carpenter. Call 303-492-6329.

If art draws your interest, visit one of the three art galleries on campus. The largest is the **University of Colorado Art Gallery** (Sibell Wolle Bldg.), housing three adjacent galleries with exhibits and educational events on significant 20th-century art. Call 303-492-8300. The entrance level of the UMC houses another gallery, and yet another resides in the inner foyer of Macky Auditorium.

CU's **Norlin Library** also hosts changing exhibits of art, photography and other material. The gallery is on the third floor, with display cases in the east and west lobbies and exhibit areas in Archives on the lower level. Special Collections on the second floor boasts more than 60,000 rare books and manuscripts, one of the major collections of its kind in the western US. Call 303-492-8302.

The Chataqua movement promoting educational experiences and enjoyment of the outdoors began in 1874, and counted 12,000 Chataqua sites nationwide in its heyday in the 1920s. Today only 20 remain, with Boulder's **Colorado Chataqua** (900 Baseline Rd) one of only three that have continuously operated. This 26-acre historic district has forty cottages, a performing arts center, dining hall, community house and more, many dating from the early 1900s. Cultural attractions include lectures, films, plays, and the Colorado Festival Orchestra. For recreation, the grounds are great for picnics, and hiking trails lead to mountain parks. Call 303-545-6924.

Turnpike/Foothills Pkwy Loop

DISTANCE: 8.0 miles, 6.7 miles off-street

ON-STREET: fairly quiet roads

SURFACE: concrete

DIFFICULTY: easy ride, with one hill

DESCRIPTION:

This route is another example of how Boulder uses its trails to knit together the city. The Foothills Parkway Trail links residents of the city's southeastern corner, and the Turnpike Trail provides easy access to the university. The Boulder Creek Trail, of course, is the 'backbone' that ties all the trails into a network.

Start your odometer at Boulder Creek and Arapahoe Rd, just west of Boulder High. Take the sidewalk along Arapahoe over the creek, then bear left then right. The path quickly climbs up University Hill, passing above Recht Field (the high school football stadium). Mercifully the hill is short, and you'll be atop the bluff in no time (keep telling yourself that).

At the top of the hill, cross University Ave at the light. The trail (now two lanes for bike traffic and one for pedestrians) follows alongside Broadway on the edge of the university. Be very careful here, as this area teems with student traffic. As you coast by, check out the sandstone buildings of CU; some are quite impressive. Follow the path across Euclid Ave (0.7 miles) and Regent Dr (1.0), both of which have traffic lights.

At 1.2 miles the trail branches. The *Broadway Trail* continues to the right under the tunnel; we'll go straight ahead, touring the southern edge of the campus. At Baseline Rd the trail veers east, crossing under 28th St/US36 (1.5). Now a left through one tunnel and a quick right through another (1.7) takes you under Baseline. To your right, a side trail heads up to *Skunk Creek*; for us, the Williams Village Towers provide a landmark as we follow the trail into open space, reaching the *Bear Creek Trail* junction at mile 2.3.

Continue straight ahead, riding on *Apache Rd* when the bike trail ends (2.5). With the turnpike on your right and undistinguished homes on your left, there is no scenery to help pass your ride, but at least little traffic shares the road. Stay on the street as it makes a 120-degree curve, turning into Thunderbird Dr and paralleling Foothills Parkway. At Sioux Dr (3.7) an overpass leads you toward the East Boulder Community Center and the *South Boulder Creek Trail* (see that writeup for details).

The bike path starts again off Thunderbird Dr (3.9). After crossing Baseline at the light (4.2), it continues to angle northwest, hidden from the Foothills Pkwy by a sound wall. The trail splits again at mile 4.8: a left turn heads you to the *Bear Creek* and *Skunk Creek Trails*, while an overpass arcs over Foothills on your right. Take the right branch, working your way up the steep overpass. (Remember to use your brakes on the way down!). Follow the trail to the left as it parallels the parkway; watch for prairie dogs in the buffer zone.

The trail crosses Arapahoe Ave at the light at mile 5.5, and reaches the Boulder Creek Trail quickly after that (5.7). Turn left and pass under the parkway to return to your starting point.

OTHER ATTRACTIONS:

On the CU campus, the **Fiske Planetarium and Science Center** (on Regent Dr) offers exhibits and lectures to university classes, school groups, and the public. The theatre uses one hundred special-effects projectors, seventy slide projectors, and two panorama systems, but the 'star' of the show is the Zeiss Mark IV projector. The adjacent **Sommers-Bausch Observatory** is open for public viewing on Friday evenings. Call 303-492-5001.

There's something fishy on campus: an aquarium. The Department of Environmental, Population, and Organismic Biology has a **teaching aquarium** open to the public while classes are not using it. The 600-square-foot center has a coral-reef ecosystem tank; an Amazon/Nile tank; a tide-pool tank; and such other wet attractions as boreal toads, horned sharks, and snowflake eels. Call 303-492-8487.

The past can be experienced at the **Boulder Museum of History** (1206 Euclid Ave). This museum has one of the largest collections (600,000 items) of local-history artifacts and photographs in the region. You can see furniture, machinery, memorabilia, and accessories from the Boulder area. Call 303-449-3464.

F*oothills Parkway Trail*

DISTANCE: 3.1 miles off-street

SURFACE: concrete

DIFFICULTY: easy, flat ride

DESCRIPTION:

The favored venue for trails in the metro area are along the region's waterways. The South Platte River and all major creeks host trails along at least part of their length and canal right-of-ways sport bike paths. Past that, highway 'ride-alongsides' prove popular. The C/E470 sports a companion trail; a short stretch parallels I-25 in Northglenn; and plans to include a path in the US36 corridor are progressing.

In Boulder, a trail flanks the Foothills Pkwy/CO157. Though obviously not as scenic as a tree-shaded creek-side trail, this trail still serves as a valuable backbone for Boulder's trail system. Using the trail lets a rider define a number of loop trips involving Boulder or South Boulder Creek.

You could unofficially start near South Boulder Rd, where the highway gets underway. Thunderbird Rd, a frontage road west of Foothills, covers the first 0.6 miles. At the north end of Thunderbird,

21

though, is where the off-street path begins.

The trail begins at the edge of the **Meadows Shopping Center**, Foothills @ Baseline Rd. Skirt the edge of the strip mall, and cross Baseline at the traffic light (0.3). The concrete trail angles northwest, hidden from the parkway by a sound wall. The trail splits at mile 0.9: a left turn takes you to the *Bear Creek* and *Skunk Creek Trails*, while an overpass arcs over Foothills on your right. Turn right, working your way up the steep overpass. (Remember to use your brakes on the way down!). Follow the trail to the left as it parallels the parkway, watching for prairie dogs in the surrounding area.

The trail crosses Arapahoe Ave at a traffic light (1.6), and then reaches the *Boulder Creek Trail* (1.8). Ignore the branches, climbing slightly then dropping to cross Pearl St (2.2) as the highway passes overhead. The trail stays low, crossing Valmont Rd at another traffic light (2.6). As it continues north, the path squeezes between the parkway and 47th St, crossing the tunnel for the *Goose Creek Trail*. It passes the trail spurs (across 47th) for *Plum Creek* and *Cottonwood trails*, and ends on 47th at Mitchell Ln (3.1).

South Boulder Creek (north)

DISTANCE: 2.1 miles, 1.4 miles off-street

ON-STREET: a short stretch on a residential dead-end

SURFACE: concrete

DIFFICULTY: easy, flat ride

DESCRIPTION:

The two main creeks running through Boulder each host off-street trails. Together, they form a network that circles much of the town. In the eastern reaches, South Boulder Creek provides a green corridor for users intent on getting their nature fix. With easy connections to Boulder Creek and to open spaces south of South Boulder Rd, it serves as a vital link in the city's bike network.

In the north, this path splits from the ***Boulder Creek Trail*** east of 55th St. From the pond, our trail breaks right, curving along the south shores to meet the feeding creek. Now heading south between the creek and an industrial park, you soon pass a bridge (mile 0.6). This spur runs 0.2 miles, allowing access to the **Stazio Recreation Complex**, 63rd St/Stazio Dr.

The main trail continues south, passing under railroad tracks and entering a wooded stretch. Here you can feel miles away from the world – except for the other riders. Enjoy the rural feel of the shaded trail, which lasts until Arapahoe Rd (1.1). Here the trail tunnels under the road, then climbs to join the thoroughfare.

Don't fret, you won't ride this busy street. Immediately west of the creek you turn south (left, but you're already on that side of the road, so you're not crossing traffic) onto *Old Tale Rd*. This quiet, dead-end road runs by tree-shaded country-club homes on large lots. Continue past McSorley Ln, ignoring the 'No Outlet' sign, to find the trail at the street's end (1.6). Cross the bridge into the open space, and immediately reach a junction. This is the *Centennial Trail*, which is a return for a lengthy loop trip.

Our trail continues south. It follows the undisturbed creek, accompanied by a gravel jogging trail. When the trail crosses the creek (1.9), it dumps you onto *Dimmit Dr*. Come out of the dead-end and turn right on *Gapter Rd*, another quiet residential road. Before Baseline Rd (2.1), the trail forms again on your right. After tunneling under Baseline, follow the concrete trail to the **trailhead**. This is a good end (or start) for the trail, or you can continue onto the south section (described in the next writeup).

S*outh Boulder Creek (south)*

DISTANCE: 3.3 miles off-street

SURFACE: dirt/crushed gravel

DIFFICULTY: easy to moderate ride

DESCRIPTION:

The South Boulder Creek path provides a nice extension to the Boulder Creek path, running upstream from their junction. As the signs state, this area of "high-quality wetlands, tall-grass prairie and cottonwood forests" is a great place to rediscover the outdoors. Though the downstream portion of the trail is a concrete path behind businesses, you can leave the paved spaces behind and travel up the creek, running through open space. You've probably seen this trail, passing under US36 at the base of the hill outside Boulder.

From the **trailhead** on Baseline, follow the concrete path into an open prairie. (A dirt walking trail runs closer to the creek, but us cyclists stick to the hard surface.) Spin through this quiet area, quickly reaching (mile 0.5) a dirt path branching to the right. To continue on the creek trail, take it - the concrete trail crosses the creek to the **East Boulder Community Center and Park**.

As we take the dirt path south, it follows the creek at a reasonable distance (a narrower dirt path, adjacent to the creek, is good for walking). This open space area is standard prairie, with a scattering of trees along the creek. It is popular, so beware of pedestrian (hiker) traffic. Also beware that portions of the trail have thicker sand and gravel or unexpected bumps.

At mile 1.0 the trail veers due east, leaving the creek to tunnel under South Boulder Rd (1.2). On the other side, follow the dirt service road west beside SBR until you reach (and cross) the creek. (If you head east along the service road, it will take you to the **Cherryvale Rd trailhead**.)

25

Pass through the gate (1.5) into the large open space. No dogs are allowed here! You now ride along a wide service road that sees no autos but many people enjoying the outdoors. There may be slightly fewer trees along this stretch, though they still line the creek banks. The trail runs through open, undeveloped grasslands, while to your right an old farm building catches the eye, framed by the Flatirons.

The trail strays a bit from the creek banks, returning to them to cross under the turnpike, US36 (1.3). Your views run all the way to the Rocky Mountain foothills, looming ever larger. The trail crosses over short boardwalks (2.8, 3.0) protecting surrounding wetlands as the trail makes a turn to the west. It finally reaches its terminus at mile 3.3, dumping into Marshall Rd as it becomes a frontage lane for CO93.

Baseline Rd

Cherryvale Rd

South Boulder Rd

36

South Boulder Creek

Marshall Rd

93

Keep in mind that the trail is constantly climbing (albeit at a very slight incline) as it crosses the open space. That fact, plus the extra effort required to pedal crushed gravel (as compared to concrete), means that this ride can give you a slightly better workout than other similar-length trails.

OPTIONS:

Are you looking for the Holy Grail of north metro bicyclists, a Denver-Boulder bikeway? As of 2008, one does not exist. However, one can connect the two with a minimum of on-street travel. From the southwest end of this trail, you can head south on lightly-traveled old Marshall Road 1.2 miles to the end at Cherryvale Rd. From here you must ride on the shoulder of busy CO 170/Marshall Rd 1.3 miles east to 66th St. A right turn on 66th (paved) takes you Coal Creek Dr (dirt road), which then heads east to the west end of the ***Coal Creek Trail*** (described in ***Broomfield/Boulder County Urban Trails***). Those last two roads run for 3.0 miles (with very little traffic), for a total connecting link of 5.5 miles.

OTHER ATTRACTIONS:

The **East Boulder Community Center and Park** offers something for all recreation tastes. Inside, you will find swimming pools, water slide, wave pool, aerobics rooms, basketball courts, weight rooms, dance and tai chi, classes, climbing wall – name it, they probably have it. Outside you can find playgrounds, volleyball pits, and racquetball, basketball and tennis courts. Tired out? Then you may just want to have a picnic lunch overlooking the pond. Call 303-413-7270.

South Boulder Creek Loop

DISTANCE: 8.7 miles, 7.4 miles off-street

ON-STREET: a residential frontage road beside
Broadway

SURFACE: concrete

DIFFICULTY: easy, flat ride

DESCRIPTION:

South Boulder Creek cuts a wide arc south and east of
Boulder proper. Because of this grand curve, and Boulder's
wonderful propensity for having bike paths wherever they can
be squeezed in (good job, Boulder!), it is fairly easy to route
out a loop trip involving this wonderful creek.

For mileage purposes, we will mark the **trailhead** on
Baseline Rd just west of Cherryvale Rd as our starting point.
From here, follow the trail (first concrete, then gravel),
through a wonderful open space area as described in the
previous writeup. You will reach old Marshall Rd at mile 3.3.

Head right on Marshall and continue past the stop
sign (the 'No Outlet' signs don't apply to bikes). The road
climbs a short hill before cresting, where it segues into a bike
path (3.5), a concrete ribbon running east of Broadway. This
path crosses Chambers Dr (3.8) and Ludlow St (4.0) on a
long, easy downhill before dumping onto Lashley Ln (4.1), a
frontage road beside Broadway. Continue northwest on
Lashley, passing a tunnel under the road (4.2) which leads to
Harlow Platts Park, and a stop sign at Hanover Ave (4.5).
When Lashley curves at Table Mesa Rd (4.7), head straight
onto the sidewalk and cross Table Mesa at the traffic light. On
the far side, the trail enters **Martin Park** to join the *Bear Creek
Trail* (4.8).

Tun right after crossing over the tunnel to reach the Bear Creek trail. Follow it through Martin Park, a well-kept grassy expanse. After crossing under Martin Dr the trail is squeezed, with concrete in the channel and fences on either side. It quickly passes under Moorhead Ave and US36 (5.4), emerging into Open Space. Cross the intersecting trail and head north through the Open Space along tree-lined Bear Creek. There has been construction going on here for some time, and the trail has been relocated.

At 5.9 miles you cross under Baseline, entering another residential area. Tight curves are your latest concern as the trail passes under Gilpin Dr (6.0), and then coasts by a set of condos. You tunnel beneath Aurora Ave at 6.4 miles and roll through

another park before this trail dead ends into an east-west trail (6.6). A left turn here will take you into the CU Research Park; for our loop, turn right, cycling through Park East Park and over Foothills Parkway.

On the east side (remember your brakes as you come off the overpass!) continue heading east on the trail provided. The path crosses Eisenhower Dr. and reaches a bridge over the ditch at mile 7.1. Now, how adventurous do you feel?

One option is to follow the path straight, following it behind a church before it bends to reach Pennsylvania Ave (7.2). Turn left, riding past many houses with distinctive, attractive gardens (during the drought, a few posted signs stating they were on well water, not using the city's drinking supplies). Of course, for a few houses the gardens are overgrown - there has to be some in every group, I suppose. At 55th, turn left and cross over the ditch to reach the *Centennial Trail* on the right.

If you prefer a less-conventional alternative, cross over the bridge spanning the ditch onto the grounds of the Eisenhower School, and follow the social trail across the field to the narrow gate cutting through the hedges. (There is one step on that sidewalk.) That puts you onto Ellsworth Pl, which you follow east until you see the *Centennial Trail* on your right (7.3). Follow that trail between a berm and the houses (no cookie-cutter homes here), passing under 55th to the earlier-mentioned junction.

Continue east, and you will see a connector (7.8) leading south along a tiny rivulet. You can take it 0.1 miles to the street, and jog just a mite to the left to reach a continuing trail - and a pleasant surprise. This trail takes you onto a greenbelt controlled by the homeowner's association (you ARE a guest here, so pay attention to the rules): an idyllic mini-park with willow and spruce trees, anchored by a necklace of quiet pools tied together by the tiny rivulet of water. On all sides, well-kept homes (all distinctive, no two alike) provide a boundary for this oasis. The main trail runs 0.2 miles before branching, and the two forks left and right run 0.2 and 0.1 to the street. You can work your way back on the road, or return by the ponds.

From the rivulet, the Centennial Trail continues east, squeezing by the Flatirons Golf Course. On your south is an open space area noted for songbirds. Soon this trail ends at South Boulder Creek (8.1), where you must turn right to get back to the trailhead. At the path's end, turn right on Gapter and follow it almost to Baseline, where the trail re-forms to take you under the street to the trailhead.

OPTIONS:

There is another option for a South Boulder Creek Loop. When the gravel trail begins (0.5), instead stay on the concrete and cross the bridge to the **East Boulder Community Center and Park**. Cross Sioux Dr, and turn left on the sidewalk, following it south to the triangle junction. Turn right on this path, and ride west between the pond and the community center. Follow this past the playground, volleyball pits, and basketball courts (and, behind them, the tennis and racquetball courts) in the park. When Sioux veers away, the trail continues into grassy East Boulder Community Park (1.1). This path ends in the parking lot of Burbank Middle School (1.3), and a left turn takes you to *Manhattan Dr* (1.4).

Now pay attention – the route has quick turns on quiet streets. Turn right on Manhattan, and immediately turn left on *Iroquois Dr*. Then immediately turn right on *Sioux Dr*, a very short street which ends yards later on Seminole Dr. Another path forms directly ahead, leading to the ramp which crosses over Foothills Pkwy. On the opposite side (1.6), the trail meets the trail described in the *Turnpike/Foothills Pkwy loop* (3.8). You then have several options to connect for a loop trip.

S *kunk Creek Trail/Table Mesa loop*

DISTANCE: 2.5-3.2 miles loop

ON-STREET: residential streets or along Table Mesa
Dr

SURFACE: concrete, asphalt

DIFFICULTY: short but strenuous

DESCRIPTION:

The National Institute of Standards and Technology (NIST, also known as the Bureau of Standards) occupies a large site on South Broadway. Though the site has several buildings to handle their important work, the density is much less than surrounding areas. With undeveloped Enchanted Mesa behind it, and Boulder Mountain Parks behind that, it serves as a great gateway to the area's open space. It also sits astride the Skunk Creek drainage, and hosts the trail serving that waterway.

You can ride the entire Skunk Creek trail from Baseline at US36, or skip the less-interesting lower creek for a loop ride in the foothills. This loop is not for those looking for a ride far from auto traffic, since a good portion is on city streets. I don't recommend it for people looking for a gentle, relaxing cruise beside a tree-shaded stream. If you're hoping for a ride with some great vistas and one that will force you to work up a sweat, then this may be your answer. Do it twice and you'll know you got your daily allotment of exercise!

For the lower stretch of trail, branch from the trail beside US36 on the southeast corner of Baseline. This branch crosses the offramp at the light, then tunnels under the freeway and the onramp. After crossing the access road, you must head through the Baseline Liquors parking lot to reach the trail. The trail crosses under the street and heads up the tamed stream. The scenery doesn't change much - drab buildings to the north, with the creek flowing at the bottom of a gully overhung by thick tall trees on the opposite bank. Finally the trail ducks under Broadway (0.5), emerging on Sunnyside Ln at Mariposa Ave.

Your other option is to stay on the trail instead of cutting through Baseline Liquor. The path follows beside Baseline Rd, reaching Broadway at mile 0.4. Cross Broadway, and head south on the trail to connect to Sunnyside Ln. You'll quickly find the creek trail.

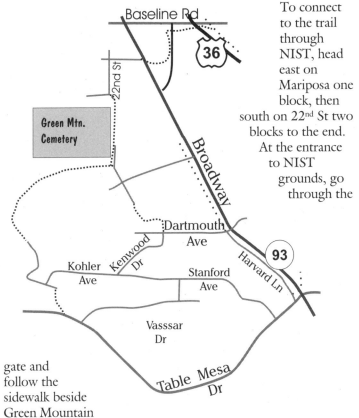

To connect to the trail through NIST, head east on Mariposa one block, then south on 22nd St two blocks to the end. At the entrance to NIST grounds, go through the gate and follow the sidewalk beside Green Mountain Cemetery. At the southeast corner of the cemetery, reach the trail heading up-creek on our loop route (1.0).

You can access the loop trail from several spots. One such spot is off Dartmouth Ave, where **Kenwood Dr** ends at a gate on the edge of NIST property. Cross through the gate, and head west on the striped asphalt road. Follow it as it veers north into the complex, becoming Compton Rd (mile 0.1). This takes you to the stop sign at Lawrence Rd (0.3), with the concrete trail just beyond this intersection. (Note that you can also turn onto Lawrence from the bikepath beside S Broadway, using that street to access this trail.)

Turn left onto the trail. It climbs along the edge of the large Green Mountain Cemetery, crossing over Kusch Rd (0.5). Now you're riding along tiny Skunk Creek, which supports a surprising amount of plants and trees. Soon you cross the creek and move into exposed spaces at the base of Enchanted Mesa. The trail continues climbing steadily, with no break in sight.

The trail dumps into Hollyberry Ln (0.9), where you can catch a quick breath. It's a teaser, because the street twists and then climbs possibly even more steeply than the trail. You finally crest (1.1) when the street turns to become **Deer Valley Rd.** (You may see cars parked here, as hiking trails accessing the Skunk Creek wilds begin at this spot.) Now you face a quick downhill and up the other side, where an asphalt trail branches to provide access to Table Mesa Dr below NCAR (1.2).

Stop and catch the views you've just earned! Then decide how you'd like to descend. For a loop trip, you can join Table Mesa Dr or follow the asphalt trail a short distance. (You'll probably opt to skip the trail after Vassar Dr anyway, since it becomes a bothersome sidewalk.) At Vassar (1.4), you have options. You can continue down *Table Mesa*, a road signed as a bike route but without bike lanes. This is a nice, high-speed downhill coast. At your last chance before reaching Broadway, turn left on *Harvard Ln* (2.6) and follow that down to *Dartmouth Ave* (3.0). You can take the ***Broadway trail*** further to *Lawrence Rd*, or you can turn left onto Dartmouth and follow that back up to *Kenwood* (3.2).

Another, shorter option is to turn left onto *Vassar* and follow neighborhood streets back to your starting point. That means turning left on *Drake St* (1.8), left on *Stanford Ave* (1.9), straight on *Kohler Dr*, and right onto *Kenwood* (2.2) to get back to Dartmouth (2.5).

OPTIONS:

At Harvard Ln and Table Mesa Dr follow the **Bear Creek Trail** north under Broadway, or head north on the **Broadway Trail** in front of NIST.

OTHER ATTRACTIONS:

Atop Table Mesa perches the **National Center for Atmospheric Research** (NCAR), also known as the 'Pink Palace'. (Does anyone remember this site from the Woody Allen movie, *Sleepers*?) This center, in a prize-winning I. M. Pei-designed building, studies basic weather and climate processes. Exhibits on the entrance level and balcony areas explain the center's mission, with scientific equipment and hands-on experiences. (This area also excels as a starting point for hiking trails along the Flatirons.) Call 303-497-1174.

Goose Creek Trail

DISTANCE: 2.4 miles off-street

SURFACE: concrete

DIFFICULTY: easy, flat ride

DESCRIPTION:

Boulder, of course, is best known for the trails along Boulder and South Boulder Creeks, but it also hosts trails along many smaller waterways. One of the newest trails, extended in 2003, is one along Goose Creek. This path runs behind the Barnes & Noble/Whole Foods complex, linking neighborhoods and businesses with the *Boulder Creek Trail*.

The upstream terminus of this trail lies at Valmont Rd and 24th St. It enters the park, quickly crossing the creek to the south side. As it exits the park, it passes by apartments, mobile homes, and an office building. At least the creek corridor gives you a bit of nature, even as stone walls rise to close in the trail and creek.

After passing under 28th St., you reach the **Mapleton ballfields** (0.6), off Mapleton Ave south of 30th St. From the park on the west side of 30th, follow the concrete trail under that main street. The path runs beside a rock-lined rivulet through a concrete-walled gully, nearly out of sight of the businesses above Goose Creek. After crossing under the railroad tracks (mile 0.8), the gulch widens, the wall disappears, and the greenbelt grows more natural. Reeds and brush now line the creek's edge.

At Foothills Pkwy (1.2), the trail forks. The branch extending south (right) provided access to the eastern part of the trail before the underpass was completed in early 2004. Now you can ignore that detour and ride under the parkway, emerging onto the *Foothills Pkwy Trail*. Jog to the right on this path, then head left to cross 47th St onto our trail (1.3).

The trail now runs behing Pearl St. Here, Pearl has none of the charm of downtown, running through an industrial-park landscape alongside a less-vegetated Goose Creek. Follow it east, where it merges with the *Wonderland Creek Trail* (1.8). Hang

right here, and ride through a prairie dog area.

After tunneling under Pearl Pkwy, the terrain changes – like going from the desert to a rain forest. A sea of reeds feeds off the backwash from the retention pond. The trail climbs above it, ending its short life at mile 2.2

OTHER ATTRACTIONS:

The **Collage Children's Museum** (2065 30th St) tweaks children's curiosity about the world with hands-on experiences, introducing them to arts and sciences, diverse cultures, and technology. They can learn about forms of energy in "Go Power"; how sound is created in "Good Vibrations"; and experience bubbles in "Bubbles Galore", among other things. Call 303-440-0053.

The Dairy Center for the Arts, housed in an old Watts-hardy Dairy building, presents diverse art exhibits in the **Dairy Gallery**. The center includes six music studios, three classrooms, a 99-seat theatre in its building. It also serves as landlord for groups such as the Boulder Philharmonic Orchestra, the Guild Theatre, and the Dairy Dance Partnership.

Goose Creek/Pearl Pkwy Loop

DISTANCE: 3.0 miles, 2.8 miles off-street

ON-STREET: on busy 30th St

SURFACE: concrete

DIFFICULTY: easy, flat ride

DESCRIPTION:

For most people, the mention of Pearl St brings to mind shopping, buskers, people-watching, sidewalk vendors, and the nationally-known Pearl St Mall. For bicyclists, though, the focus is further east, where numerous trails parallel or intersect the street. By combining trail spurs, you can make a figure-8 loop with only a short distance on city streets.

You may start this loop at the **Mapleton ballfields**, off Mapleton Ave between 28th and 30th Sts. From the park on the west side of 30th, follow the concrete trail under that main street. The path runs beside a rock-lined rivulet through a concrete-walled gully, nearly out of sight of the businesses above Goose Creek. After crossing under the railroad tracks (mile 0.2), the gulch widens, the wall disappears, and the greenbelt grows more natural. Reeds and brush now line the creek's edge.

Follow the trail through the tunnel (0.5) under Foothills Pkwy, a wonderful addition to the trail completed in January 2004. From the other side, jog right, then continue up the Goose Creek path paralleling a charm-less stretch of Pearl St. The trail, along the unadorned and fairly lifeless creek, passes a junction with the *Wonderland Creek Trail* (1.1), then crosses a prairie dog area.

After tunneling under Pearl Pkwy, the terrain changes – like going from the Sahara Desert to Brazil's rain forests. A sea of reeds feeds off the backwash from the retention pond.

The trail climbs above it, ending its short life at mile 1.5, when it dumps into the **Boulder Creek Trail**. Turn right here, and follow it past the southwest corner of the pond.

At the next junction (1.8), keep going straight, leaving the creek trail behind. You'll ride beside a feeder ditch, paralleling Pearl Pkwy. After crossing 49th St at the light (2.2) the ditch vanishes, and the trail continues beside the road, passing the business parks lining the road. You'll pass 48th St and the Foothills Park-n-Ride, under the parkway (2.4), and by Frontier Ave on your way to 30th St (2.8). Make no mistake, this is not a scenic ride – more a glorified sidewalk, but it is a great access route. At 30th, cross both directions at the light, then head north on the sidewalk. The Mapleton ballfields are directly behind the strip mall. You'll reach the entrance to the Goose Creek gully at mile 3.0.

OPTIONS:

Continue north on **Foothills Pkwy Trail** to reach the **Cottonwood & Plum Creek trails**.

Valmont Park/Wonderland Creek

DISTANCE: 1.3 miles off-street

SURFACE: concrete, crushed gravel

DIFFICULTY: easy, flat ride

DESCRIPTION:

One of the areas hosting the extensive trail development is the region north of Boulder Creek and south of Valmont Rd. Besides the newly extended *Goose Creek Trail*, Wonderland Creek and the new Valmont Park have also joined the ranks of Boulder's trails.

This section of the Wonderland Creek Trail begins at Kings Ridge Blvd and 47th St. (You can reach this directly from the *Foothills Pkwy Trail*). The trail begins on the southeast corner of the intersection, immediately running beside a pond hemmed in by houses. As you proceed down the wide wetlands strip, enjoy the trees, reeds, and other vegetations, and ignore the look-alike condos. The greenery is a breath of originality in a lockstep world.

After crossing Kings Ridge, you hit a branching trail (0.3). This short, narrow trail ends after only another tenth of a mile, dumping you onto a neighborhood street. For our ride, stay right on the main trail, running along the edge of **Christensen Park**. At the far end, the trail forks again (04.): a right turn here would take you back to the Foothills Pkwy on a sidewalk beside Valmont; our ride takes the left branch.

The trail quickly burrows under Valmont, emerging in **Valmont Park**. This new city park is only partially landscaped, with the rest given to natural vegetation. A scattering of park benches line the trail. This park does offer a few options for the trail user. Pass the first junction and proceed to the second (0.6) for your most choices. From here you can continue straight ahead, following the trail to its end (0.8) as it dumps into the *Goose Creek Trail*.

Your other option is to turn left at the second junction, onto a very short connector to a gravel path. Turning left again will take you to a parking lot for the park off Airport Rd. A right turn will let you discover the park instead. This gravel path passes over the concrete trail heading to Goose Creek, then runs along the perimeter of the

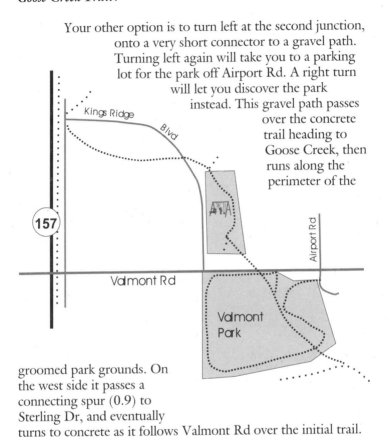

groomed park grounds. On the west side it passes a connecting spur (0.9) to Sterling Dr, and eventually turns to concrete as it follows Valmont Rd over the initial trail. It then rejoins the Wonderland Creek trail at the first junction.

OPTIONS:

Ride a stretch on the *Foothills Pkwy Trail*, or head up (or down) the *Goose Creek Trail*. You can also cross Kings Ridge Blvd at 47th to reach the *Cottonwood Trail*.

Cottonwood Trail

DISTANCE: 2.7 miles, all off-street

SURFACE: concrete, blacktop, dirt/crushed gravel

DIFFICULTY: easy, flat ride

DESCRIPTION:

In Boulder's most northeast region (not counting Gunbarrel), one trail knits together city and country. Running from a residential neighborhood and through an area zoned for business, the Cottonwood Trail ends up in rural territory on Jay Rd.

This trail begins at 47th St and Kings Ridge Blvd, across from the *Foothills Pkwy Trail*. From the northeast corner of the intersection, you can find the Cottonwood Trail on the far side of the irrigation ditch. Follow the concrete trail northeast , crossing the ditch when you reach the first junction. (Straight ahead from this point lies a parking lot.)

On the east side, turn left (right goes back to Kings Ridge). The trail here is well-shaded by the trees stealing water from the ditch. It follows the waterway, crossing over it at mile 1.1. Once the trail surface turns to blacktop (1.3), you can glimpse Hayden Lake through the trees to the right. However, there's no access (or clear view) to the lake.

A trailhead on **Independence Rd** provides easy access to the trail (1.4). Once you cross the road, the surface turns soft, a dirt path running through the edge of a large open space. This is a treat to ride, far from traffic and factories. For much of the distance, thick stands of trees accompany the stream. If not for the constant roar of Diagonal Hwy traffic, you could call it relaxing.

The trail runs close by the waterway, shaded by the big cottonwoods. It crosses a private drive at mile 1.9; please respect

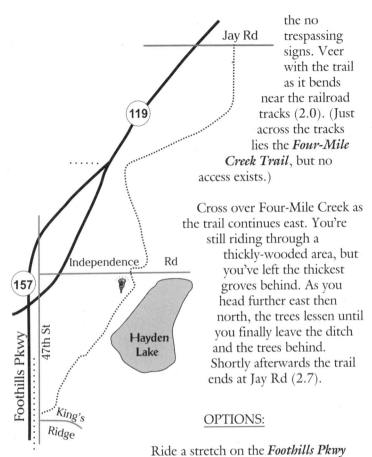

the no trespassing signs. Veer with the trail as it bends near the railroad tracks (2.0). (Just across the tracks lies the *Four-Mile Creek Trail*, but no access exists.)

Cross over Four-Mile Creek as the trail continues east. You're still riding through a thickly-wooded area, but you've left the thickest groves behind. As you head further east then north, the trees lessen until you finally leave the ditch and the trees behind. Shortly afterwards the trail ends at Jay Rd (2.7).

OPTIONS:

Ride a stretch on the *Foothills Pkwy Trail*, or cross Kings Ridge Blvd at 47th to reach the *Wonderland Creek Trail*.

Northeast Boulder loops

Boulder could be termed a 'wonderland' of opportunity for bicyclists, with its abundance of bike trails weaving through the city. It seems fitting, then, that the city should have two trails with 'wonderland' in their name. Besides Wonderland Lake in the northwest corner of town, the Wonderland Creek Greenway provides an anchor for two loop routes in Boulder's north-central region. Each travels through quiet residential areas, one inside the city limits, one largely in unincorporated areas.

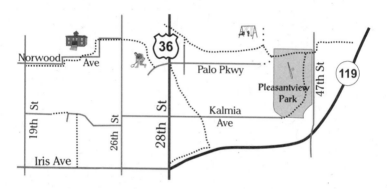

Wonderland Creek Greenway

DISTANCE: 2.9 miles, 2.1 miles off-street

ON-STREET: quite streets, or sidewalk available

SURFACE: concrete; some blacktop

DIFFICULTY: easy to moderate – one hill

DESCRIPTION:

The last time I rode this, I saved the climb up the only major hill for the very end. (This way you don't have to cross Iris Ave to reach the east-bound bike lane.) You can park at the baseball diamonds east of **Centennial Middle School** (my alma mater), making it a convenient trailhead. Follow the 'red brick road' as it parallels Norwood Ave across 26th St. Stay on the south side of Norwood as you reach 26th St, where an uncolored concrete trail passes a sign welcoming you to the Wonderland Creek Greenway. It's an easy cruise as you glide gently downhill along the concrete-jacketed creek.

At mile 0.4 you pass tennis courts as you hit Winding Trail Dr. Turn right on the quiet street, crossing 28th St at the light onto Palo Pkwy (0.5). Immediately turn right onto the sidewalk, which leaves the streets to again follow Wonderland Creek. The unleashed stream has cut into the land, and the side of the creek 'valley' hides you from the surrounding land. The terrain along the creek remains wild.

Come out of the 'ravine' to cross Kalmia Ave. On the other side, trees provide shade for the trail, a nice plus on hot summer days. Continue down the narrow greenbelt through the condo village, reaching the Longmont Diagonal Hwy in little time (1.0). Turn right on the sidewalk paralleling the highway, with a dry ditch separating you from the road.

Cross the busy US36/CO119 (28th/Diagonal) intersection at the traffic light (1.2). As you head west on Iris Ave, you can use the sidewalk or ride in the bike lane which starts after the strip mall. Follow this street past 26th St, until you reach the pedestrian light shy of 22nd St (1.7). A blacktop trail picks up here, heading north between open backyards. Again, shading trees make this an enjoyable (though short) stretch. It dead-ends onto Kalmia Ave (2.0). Head left, then straight on the trail when the street veers. This puts you back onto another branch of Kalmia (2.1), which you follow to 19th St (2.2).

Time for the grand finale! Ahead of you lies the hill that so humbled me, riding my bike to school in junior high. At least a wide sidewalk allows you to get off the street as you inch up the grade. Grind it out, and after cresting it, turn right on Norwood (2.5). Here's the red brick road again! Coast along it to the finish line at the baseball diamonds (2.9).

F*our-Mile Creek Loop*

<u>DISTANCE:</u>	2.1 miles, 1.3 miles off-street
<u>ON-STREET:</u>	mostly residential, quiet streets
<u>SURFACE:</u>	concrete
<u>DIFFICULTY:</u>	easy, flat ride

<u>DESCRIPTION:</u>

This loop trip is one of the shorter ones in Boulder. It utilizes trails running along two separate creeks, though only lasting a short distance along Wonderland Creek. More of its mileage runs along Four Mile Creek, a minor rivulet draining northeast parts of town. This trail corridor, short at the present time, presents excellent opportunities for expansion on either end, connecting to other nearby trails.

Start this loop where the Wonderland Creek Greenway crosses Kalmia Ave, just east of 28th St. Follow Kalmia east toward its dead-end, passing houses, a church, Mountain View Memorial Park (cemetery), and the Boulder Jewish Community Center. At the end (mile 0.6), turn left onto the concrete path running beside the **Pleasant View** soccer and baseball fields.

You'll promptly notice a brick landmark memorializing the site of Pleasant View School. Active from 1896-1971, this rural school was razed in 1986 and bricks used for this monument. (And a darn pleasant view it is, too, with vistas of mountains and foothills dominating the background.) It could be a very peaceful site, except for the constant roar of Diagonal Hwy traffic mere yards away.

Follow the trail along the park's edge, across the parking lot and by the restroom building (0.8). At the far end of the parking lot, the trail forks (0.9). To the right, the path runs under 47th St and the Diagonal Hwy, reverting to gravel before crossing under the CO119 (Iris Ave) entrance ramp (an extra

0.3 miles). However, the trail peters out at the edge of the railroad tracks. (Though no connection exists, the Cottonwood Trail lies on the opposite side.)

The loop trip continues left at the junction. Running by open fields with trees marking the creek to the north, the path borders the north edge of the park. At the corner (1.1), the trail forks again, with the left spur ending on the end of Palo Pkwy. Hang right instead, crossing over Four Mile Creek (hardly enough creek to worry about) into a neighborhood park, with a playground in the opposite corner.

You find another trail fork here. If you took the right spur, you could head north another 0.1 mile through the Palo Park neighborhood, or you can jog north then west, traveling 0.3 miles to another local park. For our loop trip ignore the fork, heading straight and soon leaving the park for a wetlands strip.

The trail stays close to landscaped back yards as it wends its way west. While the stream is not in a natural state, the extensive riparian vegetation almost hides the small concrete erosion control steps. After passing under 30th St, the corridor grows wilder, with bigger trees providing more shade. The Four Mile Creek Trail tunnels under 28th St (1.7), but abruptly ends on the opposite side (a dirt foot path continues to a baseball diamond). Since there is no easy connection here to 28th, I instead recommend leaving the creek trail at the previous junction, a concrete spur (1.6) that breaks left to cross the stream and connect to *Paseo del Prado*.

Follow the street south by condos, crossing Palo Pkwy (1.7) onto the sidewalk on the south side. Take this sidewalk west toward the traffic light. Just before reaching it (1.8), turn south (left) onto the Wonderland Creek Greenway trail. Follow this along the creek until it reaches Kalmia (2.1), your starting point.

Wonderland Lake Loop

DISTANCE: 3.6 miles, 3.1 miles off-street

ON-STREET: thru quiet neighborhoods

SURFACE: crushed gravel and concrete

DIFFICULTY: easy to moderate – one steep hill

DESCRIPTION:

The Wonderland Lake neighborhood in north Boulder is permeated with a web of bike trails. You can link them in a variety of ways, constructing an intricate series of interlocking loops. For this book, I will highlight one possible trail, a route which links the lake with the **Foothills Community Park**.

A southern spur of this trail begins at the bend of 4th St/Kalmia Ave. It heads north on what would have been 4th, and starts as essentially a private driveway shared by two exclusive houses on either side. Once the official driveways part, the concrete trail continues on to reach Linden Ave at mile 0.1. After crossing the street, the left branch of the path ends quickly; turn right instead and immediately head left on *Wonderland Hill Ave*. Our official loop route starts on the off-street trail on your left, opposite Linden Park Dr.

You start by climbing a short hill on aging concrete. Expensive homes perch on the hillsides in front of you. Once you crest the hill, closer homes crowd in on both sides. At mile 0.1 we hit the first trail fork; we'll take the left fork for our loop route. (The right branch runs 0.1 to the 'circle rib' junction we'll hit on the return.)

You're now navigating a gentle downhill, passing connections to the side streets. Cross Poplar Ave, continuing straight on the trail into Wonderland Lake Park. As the trail forks (0.4), bear left, and the trail will soon turn to crushed gravel. This path takes you on the west side of the lake, with open land on either side. North of the lake, the trail forks again (0.7) – choose the left branch to investigate the rest of the trail. I know, you're facing a steep hill, but it doesn't last long. (You can shorten the loop by turning right.) The view from the top, with the lake splayed below you and barren foothills to your side, is your reward.

The gravel path continues north through a wildlife sanctuary, reaching **Foothills Community Park** at mile 1.1. This new park features roller hockey rinks, two playgrounds, and community gardens. Take the turn into the park, then head left on the concrete path to circle the large, grassy area - maybe you will see people practicing hang gliding. The path will pass a connection to Cherry Ave (1.4) before reaching the park buildings. As you continue circling the park, take the 'exit' on the south side (1.5) before the trail goes back to your entrance point.

On the southeast side of the park, take Locust Ave to 9th St, and turn south for two streets to Utica St. A right turn will take you back to the trail (2.1) just past Cottage Ln. (If you turned right at the base of the big hill, you would rejoin our loop here.) Be sure to look closely for the trail start, since it is slightly hidden. It starts under a tree by the speed bump. The trail dives back into the lush growth, then turns right (2.3) to cross over the earthen dam. Before reaching Quince Cr (2.5), turn right onto the concrete south side trail.

This path runs between houses and the lake, with intermittent shade from trees. Ignore the first left spur, then bear left when you reach the loop (2.7) around the small, developed park. (The path continues west to the junction where we entered the lake park.) Follow this with a left as the trail 'T's off, as the cement leads back to Poplar. Directly across the street, four steps lead to the raised sidewalk.

Climb along this path, quickly hitting the 'circle rib' juction (2.8). A right turn goes back to the first trail fork, but we turn left. Now we have another –actually, seven choices. The path heading left passes six spurs ('ribs') as well as continuing forward. Each of the seven paths take you back to Wonderland

Hill Ave, or to cul-de-sacs off that street. The first left spur runs through a finely landscaped strip, while many of the rest are more wild.

Once you hit *Wonderland Hill*, a right turn will take you back to your starting point. (You'll have to climb a slight bit first.) At the corner of Wonderland Hill and Moffit Ct (where the straight-ahead path hits the street), you'll notice a concrete path heading east. Don't take it for this loop, – it ends on 28th St, across from the end of Norwood Ave.

OPTIONS:

Take the spur at Moffit Ct and Wonderland Hill Ave east, then east on Norwood Ave 0.5 miles to connect with the *Wonderland Creek Greenway Loop*. For more open space, keep going straight on the gravel path instead of turning into Foothills Community Park and explore *Four Mile Creek West*.

Foothills Open Space/4-Mile Creek west

DISTANCE: 1.3 miles, 1.1 miles off-street

ON-STREET: a short stretch on a residential street

SURFACE: crushed gravel and concrete

DIFFICULTY: easy to moderate – one steep hill

DESCRIPTION:

Boulder is known for both its paved/crushed gravel bike trails, and for its mountain bike paths. Rarely do the two meet, but in north Boulder one 'road bike' trail actually morphs into a more challenging route for wide-tire bikes.

A good trailhead for this ride is the **Foothills Community Park** at Cherry Ave/ 7th St. If you start here, work your way to the gravel trail snaking through the open space along the foothills. The gravel path, accessible to all bikes, continues north through the wildlife sanctuary. Enjoy the feeling of remoteness, though you never lose sight of homes.

This trail reaches a trailhead on Lee Hill Rd after 0.5 miles. If you have a wide-tired bike, you can continue across the road and pick up the trail there. It parallels roads going in for the new subdivision, still an easy crushed gravel surface. When it reaches the end of the subdivision, though, rocks and grades push it beyond the reach of skinny-tire bikes. If you have a mountain bike, you could continue, reaching an underpass tunneling beneath US36 (3.0) and eventually the Boulder Reservoir, according to signs.

Other riders still have a trail to explore. From the Lee Hill trailhead, head east to *6th St*, and turn right. This turns into Zania Ave, which you take to the end (0.0). The *4-Mile Creek Trail* now begins on your right. Follow it across Yellow Pine Ave, when it enters the open space.

This concrete path runs through the open space (you can see the houses surrounding Foothills Park ahead of you, then enters a less-scenic corridor, running behind storage units and by a trailer park. After tunneling under Broadway, the trail ends on Rosewood St.

OPTIONS:

From the Foothills Park, head south to enjoy the trail network around *Wonderland Lake*.

Off the South Boulder loop

Twin Lakes Trail

DISTANCE:	1.9 miles off-street
ON-STREET:	cross quiet neighborhood streets
SURFACE:	crushed gravel; concrete at the ends
DIFFICULTY:	easy, flat trail

DESCRIPTION:

At the eastern edges of Boulder, partway to Longmont off the Diagonal Hwy, lie the neighborhoods of Gunbarrel. This subdivision, part in and part out of city limits, has served as a city outpost for decades. Though it seems to be an 'island' surrounded by county lands, it is actually connected to the rest of the town by a narrow, undeveloped corridor running west from Boulder Reservoir. You can't drive here from the rest of town without leaving town first ... you may be able to do it on a mountain bike, though (see the extension of the Foothills Open Space/4-Mile Creek West Trail).

The Twin Lakes Trail runs through county lands in the Gunbarrel region, running adjacent to municipal lands for part of its length (and actually cutting a corner of town near the end). You can find the western end of the path at the corner of Orchard Creek Cir & Ln, a block west of Spine Rd. The trail starts out as a concrete ribbon winding through a wild corridor between homes, anchored by a small unfettered creek. However, this first stretch effectively ends a few yards shy of Spine Rd, petering out into a dirt social trail that connects to the street (mile 0.2). Cross the street, then cross a few yards of grass or dirt to catch the rebirth of the trail, which begins again by a fence bordering the street.

The narrow, winding dirt path hugs the tiny creek through a shady, peaceful strip which seems more relaxed than the first portion. Homes and condos border the trail on either side, but they don't hammer you with the dull monotony of many new developments. Here, variety rules, with some sporting bright pink or purple motifs. Be careful of the two residential streets you cross on the path; the curbs are nasty. At the first (Wellington Rd) jog left to cross the creek and find the trail at the edge of a **community park**.

After crossing Robinson Ln (0.6), the terrain opens up a bit. You cross under 63rd St (0.8) in a concrete tunnel, but the trail reverts to dirt as it passes through a wide grassy strip. At mile 0.9 the trail

forks. The right-most branch takes you across Twin Lakes Rd at mile 1.0 (watch the curbs), then turns into a concrete sidewalk squeezed between a pond and houses. It ends shortly afterwards in a large vacant field (1.2).

Instead, bear left at the trail fork and cross the bridge. Now follow the creek, ignoring a right branch (1.1) heading back to Twin Lakes Rd. The land opens up, then changes again as the trees close in, putting you into a virtual forest. It remains that way as you pass by the twin lakes the tract was named for. (You can't actually *see* the ponds, as they remain out of sight behind the berms.) This rural-feeling stretch is a nice escape from the city's bustle.

When the trail dumps you onto Twin Lakes Rd (1.5), the ride is not done. Turn right, and cross the street to catch a concrete path by the tennis courts. The trail forks again (1.6), and we'll take a left to follow the trail by a large drainage ditch. To the left, condos line the path, but few fences close them off. Finally the trail curves around to end at Williams Fork Tr (1.9).

OTHER ATTRACTIONS:

The Gunbarrel area offers a few sites of interest once you're through with your brush with nature. If you'd like to see a faster mode of transportation, check out the racing cars assembled in the **Shelby American Collection**, 5020 Chapparal Ct (open Saturday afternoons). The 10,000-square-foot museum is dedicated to Shelby Cobra, Shelby GT 350, Ford GT 40, and other cars associated with driver Caroll Shelby. Call 303-516-9565.

Have you seen the Leanin' Tree greeting cards in your local stores? The company's corporate headquarters, 6055 Longbow Dr, houses one of the nation's largest privately-owned collections of western art. More than 200 paintings and over 80 bronze sculptures are displayed in the **Leanin' Tree Museum of Western Art**. This facility attracts approximately forty thousand visitors each year. Call 303-530-1442.

Ready for some refreshments? Check out the **Visitor Center** at **Celestial Seasonings**, the nation's largest specialty tea company. This center has exhibits on the company, a tea-tasting bar, a café and herb garden, and a gift shop. You can sip tea while looking through the windows overlooking the tea production area, or take a tour. Call 303-581-1202.

*C*ottontail/Homestead Trail

DISTANCE: 2.8 miles, all off-street

SURFACE: crushed gravel (concrete only at start)

DIFFICULTY: easy to moderate

DESCRIPTION:

On the northeastern frontier of Boulder, Gunbarrel Estates hangs half-in, half-out of the city limits. With open fields and farmlands bounding it, it provides an ideal setting for a bike trail. Not only is there a wonderful trail tracing the northern perimeter of the subdivision, a few years ago it connected to the trail system in Niwot — and long-range plans include connecting that system to Longmont.

The southwest end of the Homestead Trail is on Lookout Road, adjacent to the canal. From the sidewalk paralleling the road, a concrete trail branches to follow the ditch. A housing development holds the ground on your right, but views (if you can see past the trees lining the canal) to the mountains keep you company to the west.

When the concrete ends (0.2), you veer from the houses. A large grassy hill now borders the trail, giving you open space between you and civilization. The soft-surface way continues along the canal. Cross over the canal at mile 0.6, and you feel even more remote for a short time. (This stretch can be shady, which means ice and snow can last during the winter, and mud could hang in during rainy springs.) At mile 1.0, a connector takes you to Idylwild Tr.

As you continue along the trail, an industrial park sprouts on your left. With fewer trees along the canal, your views to the north extend to the traffic racing by on the Diagonal Highway. (I'm sure they're not having as much fun as you are.) Once you reach 71st St (1.3), the Homestead Trail ends, and the Cottontail Trail picks up across the road. That trail curves north a bit, running through a corridor between houses.

When the trail again angles east, you again have open land to your right. The canals (which have become dueling ditches) and the trail follow the edge of the neighborhood, with once again adundant trees fed from the leaking canal water. You'll pass another connecting trail at mile 1.7, leading you back to Gunbarrel Rd.

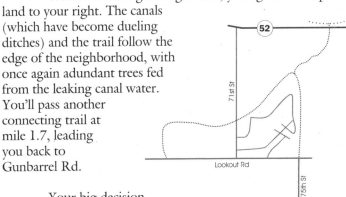

Your big decision comes at mile 2.1, at the northeast corner of the housing tract. Junction! If you turn right, the crushed gravel trail heads nearly straight south, climbing gently in the open space between the houses and farm land. The hills on your left limit your views. At the end of the mild slope, the trail ends (2.8) at Lookout Rd, right where 75th St dead-ends into it.

The 'new' (circa 2004) trail heads left from the junction. At first, you're squeezed between the canal bores, but a bridge takes you over one of them into wide-open terrain. The trail again turns north, and soon runs underneath CO52 to connect to the **_Monarch Trail_** in Niwot (see **_Northern Colorado Urban Trails_** for more information). (As typical, the trail turns concrete to get you under the road.) You can continue into Niwot, or return the way you came. If you don't feel complete without fighting a little auto traffic, you can turn left on the Monarch Trail to get back to the road, follow CO 52 west to 71st, and take that south back to the trail. (A round-trip of Cottontail, CO 52, and 71st takes 3 miles.)

E*ast Boulder Trail*

<u>DISTANCE:</u>   4.9-6.1 miles, all off-street

<u>SURFACE:</u>   crushed gravel

<u>DIFFICULTY:</u> easy to moderate

<u>DESCRIPTION:</u>

    People have long considered Boulder to be a hotbed of cycling. (Think back to the old Red Zinger races!) Thus, it comes as no surprise that the county should host a wealth of bike trails. One of the nicer trails, managed by the city though running through county lands well east of the city limits, opens up farmland, hillsides, ponds, and an interesting geographical/historical feature – the White Rock Cliffs.

    The trail is served by three trailheads. In the north, a dirt lot on **95<u>th</u> St** 1.4 miles north of Valmont Rd provides parking for several vehicles. 0.6 miles west of 95th on **Valmont**, another trailhead allows easy access to the Teller Farm Open Space. (This is named for Henry Teller, who founded the Colorado Central Railroad, was one of Colorado's two first senators, and served as the Secretary of the Interior for President Chester A. Arthur.) The chief trailhead, with restrooms, lies at the end of a short access road off **Arapahoe Rd**, 2.2 miles east of 75th St. We'll log mileage from there.

    The dirt-and-gravel trail runs east, heading for Teller Lake. You can reach the lake (a wildlife preserve) by continuing straight, but the East Boulder Trail veers left to drop behind/below the reservoir. It cruises on a very slight downhill, passing through gates (remember to close them behind you) as it crosses private property. After a short distance with houses to the east, it enters a larger open-space: the Teller Farm area. Local farmers and ranchers lease this land from the city, preserving the area's rich agricultural heritage. (This helps maintain Boulder's water rights, preserves natural values, and (best of all?) restricts development.

Once you hit the central trailhead, you have an option. You can turn left on *Valmont*, or you can cross the parking lot to find a minor connector heading west. In either case, the main trail picks up again on the north side of Valmont (2.3), heading into the White Rocks leg. (NOTE that this section is marked as a 'no-dogs' area.)

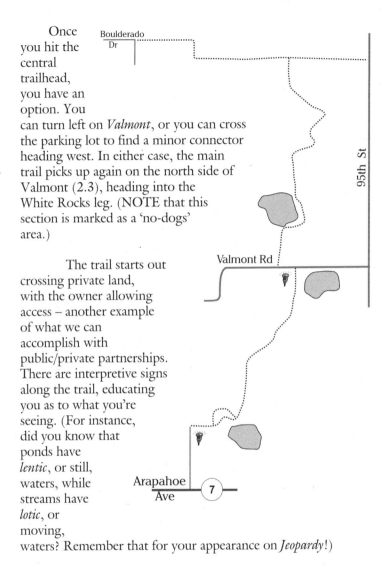

The trail starts out crossing private land, with the owner allowing access – another example of what we can accomplish with public/private partnerships. There are interpretive signs along the trail, educating you as to what you're seeing. (For instance, did you know that ponds have *lentic*, or still, waters, while streams have *lotic*, or moving, waters? Remember that for your appearance on *Jeopardy!*)

The trail passes by an award-winning pond. Flatirons Gravel won the award (from the Wildlife Society and the National Sand & Gravel Assn) for their reclamation efforts here. By mining the gravel in only one section each winter, and reclaiming it the following spring, they managed to mitigate erosion, and also kept weeds from invading and taking over. Good job!

As you cross Boulder Creek, you can see the White Rock Cliffs to the west. A remnant of the ancient seas that

covered this land, these were used by Native Americans as a buffalo jump. Soon, though, your attention is diverted by the fact that the trail is rising (3.4). Now it rises steeply across the ridge, then turns (3.7) to climb more slowly and steadily.

The scenery continues to help the distance drop off. When you can't see the foothills, massive homes attract your attention. Even when the homes fade from sight, the tight turns taking you around the surrounding, scrub-filled hills holds interest. The trail tops off, then drops and climbs again. You finally crest out at mile 4.3, then cross a private drive and hit your northern junction (4.4). A right turn here will take you to the northern trailhead (4.9). Watch your speed, as you drop along a trail that can get rutted.

A left turn at the northern junction takes you into Gunbarrel Farms. For the first mile of this trail, you climb fairly steadily and (at times) steeply. (Again, be careful on your return. The surface is uneven enough to keep you from coasting with no braking.) The scenery here is less spectacular, with the Rockies mostly hidden from view until you crest the hill. At that point you have another half-mile or so, cruising down into Heatherwood at the corner of Boulderado Dr & Cambridge St. This extra leg runs 1.7 miles between the junction and the street. You can continue west on *Boulderado Dr*, and catch a connecting gravel trail (1.9) which runs to 75th St.

OPTIONS:

You can head north on the sidewalk beside 75th St for 0.5 miles to connect to the ***Cottontail Trail.***

$\mathbf{A}$ *bout the Author --*

Glen Hanket was raised in Boulder, Colorado when it was still a sleepy college town. A software engineer by trade, he writes books and gives speeches and slide shows on bicycling, walking, National Parks, and the evils of litter in his 'spare time.'

Glen is perhaps best known for his LitterWalk -- a hike he took with his wife (shortly after their wedding) from Maine to Oregon, picking up four tons of litter along the way. His adventure is recounted in the book, ***Underwear by the Roadside***, available from CAK Publishing or from bookstores across the country. The sequel to that book, ***Wow! What a Ride***, tells of running with the Olympic Torch, appearing on *To Tell the Truth*, bicycling from coast-to-coast, and more. It is available as a free download at www.bikepaths.com.

You may order any of our fine bicycle trail guides on the web at www.bikepaths.com. You can also use the convenient order form below.

Please send me:

_____ Underwear by the Roadside ($10.00)
_____ WOW! What a Ride! (free download online)
_____ Take A Bike! 3rd edition ($14.00)
Take A Bike! Series ($7.00 each)
_____ Boulder Urban Trails
_____ Broomfield/Boulder County Urban Trails
_____ Adams County Urban Trails
_____ Westminster Urban Trails
_____ Jefferson County Central Urban Trails
_____ Jefferson County South Urban Trails
_____ North Denver/Aurora Urban Trails
_____ Denver/Platte Triangle Urban Trails
_____ Arapahoe County South Urban Trails
_____ Highlands Ranch Area Urban Trails
_____ Douglas County Central Urban Trails
_____ Northern Colorado Urban Trails
_____ Southern Colorado Urban Trails
_____ Mountain Resorts Urban Trails
_____ Western Colorado Urban Trails

I am enclosing the specified amount (less 10% for orders of 2 books or more), plus shipping and handling of $1.50 for one book/$2.25 for two books/ $3.00 for 3 or more books. Colorado residents, please add 3% tax. Send check or money order to:
    CAK Publishing
    PO Box 953
    Broomfield, CO 80038
Allow up to three weeks for delivery.

SHIP TO: _____

ADDRESS: _____

CITY/STATE: _____

                          ZIP: _____
PHONE: _____